D0996525

SIMPLY
GOOD TASTE

Published in Great Britain by Simon & Schuster
UK Ltd, 2009
A CBS Company

Simon & Schuster UK Ltd
1st Floor, 222 Gray's Inn Road, London WC1X 8HB

First published 2007
This edition published 2009

ISBN 978-1-84737-476-9

1 3 5 7 9 10 8 6 4 2

Edited by: Chris Catlin and Iain Middleton
Photographed by: Richard Faulks
Designed and produced by: Mik Baines

Printed and bound in China

Good Taste, 19 Lake Road, Keswick, Cumbria CA12 5BS

www.simplygoodtaste.co.uk

PETER SIDWELL'S

SIMPLY GOODTASTE

GREAT FOOD FOR FRIENDS AND FAMILY

SIMON &
SCHUSTER

LONDON · NEW YORK · SYDNEY · TORONTO

Welcome to my world, a world of mouth-watering food and breathtaking scenery.

Where the freshness and flavour of the great local produce here in Cumbria and the Lakes combine with the style and flair of Mediterranean cuisine. Where I'm just as happy preparing something special for hungry hikers and hill walkers as for cosmopolitan gourmets. It might be a wrap of Parmesan chicken with wild garlic I've picked myself. Or home-baked focaccia toasted with our lovely local brie. Call in at *Good Taste*, my café in Keswick, and it could be breakfast frittata with Cumberland sausages... or maybe West Coast mackerel with lemon crostini.

The longer I live here, the more inspiration I get from my surroundings.

Whether I'm fly fishing for trout and salmon, or taking a walk in the hills with my wife Emma and our dog, I'm always dreaming up new food ideas. Depending on the time of year, I'll be looking for wild mushrooms, or wood sorrel, or maybe some juicy ripe blackberries in a roadside hedgerow. By evening we could be trying out a blackberry and lemon sorbet. With me, there's always a link with food. The same is true when I'm travelling abroad. I visit Italy twice a year and just love to bring new ideas back home to Keswick.

This cook book is all about blending those ideas together to make everyday eating more exciting - and everyday cooking more fun. So if you like the sound of local lamb with mint couscous instead of mint sauce, or poached eggs with caramelised pancetta instead of baked beans, this is your kind of book.

My world is my kitchen. **Step inside!**

Contents

OUT& ABOUT

BOOTS ON. WATERPROOF ZIPPED.
PACK SOME SNACKS, LET'S GO!

Great food always seems to taste better in the open air. That's why many of my recipes are designed to be eaten and enjoyed outdoors – and here in the Lake District there's no better table than by a lake or on one of the fell tops.

BAKED SANDWICH

THESE FRESHLY BAKED ROLLS WITH SAVOURY FILLINGS ARE JUST PERFECT FOR A KID'S LUNCHBOX OR A PICNIC!

Here's how...

Place the flour, yeast, sugar and salt in a bowl and mix, making a well in the centre. Pour in the water and olive oil. Follow the instructions for Focaccia Bread (page 31), but leave out the sea salt and roll out into a 1cm thick rectangle.

For the tomato and mozzarella filling, spread the pesto over the dough. Top with the sun-blushed tomatoes and pine nuts. Tear up the mozzarella and scatter over the top. Roll up the dough towards you to form a Swiss roll. Cut into 5cm thick slices and place on a greased baking tray. Leave to prove for 20 minutes in a warm place. Brush with beaten egg and bake for 15 minutes at 220°C.

For the other fillings, spread the ingredients on the dough in the same way before rolling and slicing.

Ingredients

Makes 10 rolls

500g strong flour
7g dried yeast
1 tbsp sugar
1 tbsp salt
300ml warm water
50ml olive oil
1 egg, beaten, for glaze

Tomato and mozzarella

4 tbsp pesto
200g sun-blushed tomatoes
2 tbsp pine nuts
2 x 125g mozzarella balls

Ham and cheese

2 tbsp Dijon mustard
8 slices air-dried ham
200g Emmenthal cheese

Tapenade (facing page)

100g tapenade (olive paste)
2 x 125g mozzarella balls
2 sprigs rosemary (leaves only)
1 tbsp sea salt

Chorizo and cheese

150g chorizo
100g Manchego cheese
20 olives, pitted

JAPANESE BEEF WRAP

THIS IS A GREAT WAY TO USE UP THE LAST FEW SLICES OF ROAST BEEF THAT YOU COULDN'T QUITE MANAGE FOR SUNDAY LUNCH.

Here's how...

Pour the soy sauce and both the oils into a mixing bowl and add in the finely sliced chilli and ginger. Add a few grated rasps of garlic, which will be quite strong as it won't be cooked.

Shred the beef and add to the mixture together with the bean sprouts, spring onions and coriander. Mix together.

Lay out the wraps, top with a portion of the beef filling and form a roll. You can spread a little softened butter along the inside of the outer edge of the tortilla to help stick it down.

Ingredients

Serves four

50ml soy sauce
50ml groundnut oil
1 tsp sesame oil
½ red chilli
1 thumb of ginger, peeled
1 clove garlic
4 to 6 slices of cold roast beef
300g bean sprouts, rinsed and drained
4 spring onions, thinly sliced
1 handful fresh coriander, chopped
4 tortilla wraps
1 knob butter, softened

ROASTED VEGETABLE AND FETA POCKET

BRING A PACKED LUNCH TO LIFE WITH THESE FRAGRANT FLAVOURS. PERFECT FOR A DAY'S WALKING ON THE FELLS!

Here's how...

Combine the dressing ingredients in a jar, replace the top and shake well.

Cut the courgettes, pepper and onion into chunks and dress with the olive oil and a smashed garlic clove.

Heat a dry grill pan over a high heat and chargrill the vegetables to your liking.

When the vegetables have some good colour and are still firm, remove from the heat and season with salt and pepper. Allow to cool and toss in the dressing.

Break up the Feta into the vegetables followed by the chopped mint.

Cut each pitta open along one side to create a pocket. Spoon the mixture into the pockets. Don't forget the liquid from the bottom of the bowl as it will be packed with flavour.

Fold the pittas up in foil so nothing can escape. Now you're ready to pack your rucksack!

Ingredients

Serves four

Dressing for vegetables

1 tbsp balsamic vinegar
1 tbsp honey
1 tbsp extra virgin olive oil
squeeze of lemon juice

2 courgettes
1 salad pepper
1 red onion
30ml olive oil
1 clove garlic
salt and pepper
100g Feta
10 leaves fresh mint, chopped
4 pitta breads

SOFFRITTO SOUP

SOFFRITTO IS ITALIAN FOR THE COMBINATION
OF FIVE VEGETABLES USED IN THIS RECIPE. IT'S
THE BASIS FOR MANY ITALIAN DISHES – AND
HERE IT ENDS UP IN YOUR THERMOS AS A
HEARTY SOUP.

Here's how...

Dice the vegetables and garlic. Heat a large
saucepan with a drizzle of olive oil, add the
vegetables and stir over a gentle heat for five
minutes. Add the flour, tomato purée and
sugar and mix well. Pour in the white wine and
vegetable stock, add the rosemary and bay
leaf and simmer for 40 minutes.

Wash the tinned beans, add to the soup and
reheat. Remove the bay leaf and season with
salt, pepper and wild garlic (optional). Serve or
pour into your flask.

Chef's tip This soup is even better if you
add a tablespoon of fresh pesto just as you
serve it.

Ingredients
Serves four

1 onion
1 leek
2 carrots
4 sticks celery
3 cloves garlic
olive oil
2 tbsp flour
2 tbsp tomato purée
1 tbsp sugar
150ml white wine
1 litre vegetable stock
1 sprig rosemary,
   chopped
1 bay leaf
1 x 400g tin mixed
   Italian beans
salt and pepper
wild garlic leaves
   (if in season)

ESPRESSO FRUIT BREAD

THIS IS BASED ON A TRADITIONAL YORKSHIRE FRUIT BREAD RECIPE GIVEN TO ME BY MY WIFE'S GRANNY. I JUST TWEAKED IT SLIGHTLY TO SUIT MY STYLE OF COOKING.

Here's how...

Soak the chopped dates in the espresso for 10 minutes or so until the liquid is absorbed and the dates have softened.

Rub together the flour and butter, then add the sugar. Whisk the eggs and add to the mixture.

Pour in the soaked dates and coffee and add the hazelnuts. Finally add the milk and mix well.

Divide the mixture between two greased 2lb loaf tins lined with greaseproof paper.

Bake for an hour at 130°C then reduce the heat and bake for another hour at 100°C.

Ingredients

Serves four

700g chopped dried dates
six shots (200ml) of espresso or strong coffee
400g self-raising flour
250g butter
250g caster sugar
4 large eggs
100g whole hazelnuts
4 tbsp milk

ROASTED PECAN BROWNIES
A GREAT ONE FOR CHOCOHOLICS – AND NUTCASES!

Here's how...

Preheat the oven to 180°C. Place the pecans on a baking tray and cook for 10 minutes until crisp.

Break the chocolate into small chunks, setting aside a few chunks for later. Place the rest of the chocolate and the butter in a mixing bowl over a pan of simmering water. Allow to melt.

In a separate bowl whisk the sugar and eggs together until light and fluffy. Add the egg mixture to the chocolate and butter, sieve the flour into the mixture and fold in carefully. Finally add the orange zest and espresso.

Pour the mixture into a lined and greased 20 x 30cm baking tray. Sprinkle with the toasted pecans and the last few chunks of chocolate.

Bake for 35 minutes at 185°C. The brownies are cooked when the mix starts to crack. Remove from the oven and leave to cool. If you wish, you can dust with icing sugar. When cool, cut into squares and serve.

Ingredients

Serves eight

100g pecans
350g dark chocolate
250g butter
150g sugar
3 large eggs
100g self-raising flour
zest of 1 orange
1 shot of espresso
icing sugar (optional)

FOCACCIA BREAD

I JUST LOVE MAKING BREAD, ESPECIALLY THIS FOCACCIA.
USUALLY I BAKE IT FIRST THING IN THE MORNING BEFORE MY
CAFÉ OPENS. THE IDEA COMES FROM FRANCESCO, AN ITALIAN
FRIEND WHO SHOWED ME HOW IT'S DONE.

Here's how...

Place the two flours into a bowl and mix, using your hand like a claw. Make a well in the middle and add the sugar and yeast. Pour in the olive oil and warm water. There's no precise measurement for the water, I've given only a rough guide. On a warmer day you might need a splash more.

Stick both your hands in and mix the dough. When the dough comes together – and away from the bowl – transfer it to a floured work surface sprinkled with a little sea salt.

Continue to knead the dough by holding it with one hand and pushing it away with the other. When it has stretched away pull it back toward the other hand and repeat the process. The dough is ready after about 5 minutes when it becomes smooth and shiny. Place the dough in a bowl and cover with cling film. Rest in a warm place for 1 hour to double in size. The airing cupboard is great or, if it's warm, outside in the sun.

Next, place the dough on a lightly floured surface and knead for 2 or 3 minutes more. Use a rolling pin to roll the dough into your desired shape – one large focaccia or smaller, individual ones. Place the rolled-out dough into a baking tray, using your fingers to push holes into the dough. Leave somewhere warm to prove for a further 20 minutes.

When the dough has risen again, decorate the bread with small sprigs of rosemary, scatter with sea salt and drizzle over plenty of olive oil. At this stage you can also push cherry tomatoes (not shown) into holes in the dough.

Bake in the oven for 20 minutes at 220°C or until golden. Check by lifting up the bread – it's ready if it is golden brown underneath.

Ingredients

Serves four to six

250g strong white
    bread flour
250g '00' pasta flour
1 tbsp sugar
7g dried yeast
6 tbsp extra virgin
    olive oil, plus extra
    for drizzling
300ml warm water
1 tbsp coarse
    sea salt
4 sprigs rosemary
12 cherry tomatoes
    (optional)

SWEET GARLIC CHUTNEY AND LOCAL BRIE ON FOCACCIA BREAD

Here's how...

Heat the olive oil in a thick bottomed pan and fry the onions until soft. Add the white wine vinegar, sugar, thyme and turmeric. Simmer until the sugar dissolves.

Peel and chop the garlic, add to the pan and simmer for a further 20 minutes.

Taste the chutney. If it is too sweet, add a splash more vinegar. Season with salt and pepper. This chutney is all about personal taste so make it your own!

Allow to cool, transfer to a glass jar, seal and refrigerate. It will keep for up to 1 month in the fridge.

To make the sandwich

Cut open the focaccia bread and spread with the garlic chutney. Slice the Brie and place it on the bread. Top with selected rocket leaves. If you like, finish with a squeeze of lemon juice over the rocket.

Ingredients

Makes two small jars

Garlic chutney
50ml olive oil
2 large white onions, finely chopped
50 ml white wine vinegar
300g sugar
4 sprigs thyme
1 tsp turmeric
4 bulbs garlic
salt and pepper

focaccia bread (page 31)
Brie (Keldthwaite Gold if available)
rocket leaves
lemon juice (optional)

COURGETTE AND PESTO QUESADILLAS

A SAVOURY WRAP THAT'S JUST GREAT FOR PERSUADING KIDS TO EAT AND ENJOY VEGETABLES.

Here's how...

Preheat the oven to 180°C.

Spread the pesto (page 49) over the tortilla wraps.

Cover with half the torn mozzarella then grate the courgettes over the top.

Add the last of the torn mozzarella, season well, and top, sandwich-style, with another tortilla wrap.

Place the quesadillas straight on to the oven shelf and bake for 10 minutes until crisp.

Ingredients

Serves four

4 tbsp pesto (page 49)
8 tortilla wraps
2 x 125g soft mozzarella
3 courgettes
salt and black pepper

KIDS' LUNCH BOX
THIS COMBINATION OF SNACKS IS A QUICK AND EASY WAY TO GET KIDS EATING HEALTHY AND EXCITING FOOD.

HEALTHY CHICKEN NUGGETS

Ingredients
Serves four

8 slices wholemeal bread
2 x 200g chicken breasts
1 pear
2 tbsp tomato ketchup
3 eggs
4 tbsp plain flour
3 tbsp milk
2 tbsp vegetable oil

Here's how...
Blend the bread into breadcrumbs and place in a bowl.

Dice the chicken and place in a food processor. Pulse until smooth. Squeeze off any excess juice.

Grate the pear and add to the chicken. Add the ketchup and one egg yolk and pulse until smooth.

Shape the nuggets with a tablespoon dipped in water to stop the mixture sticking.

Roll the nuggets in flour, then the remaining eggs (beaten with the milk) and finally the breadcrumbs.

Drizzle a little oil onto a non-stick baking tray and bake the nuggets for 15 minutes at 180°C until firm.

MANGO HEDGEHOG

Ingredients

Serves four

2 mangoes

Here's how...

Cut the mangoes down the middle either side of the stone.

With a sharp knife score the mango flesh in a criss-cross pattern, making sure you don't cut through the outer skin. When the mango is pushed open the neatly cut cubes of fruit are presented ready to eat.

KEBABS

Ingredients

Serves four

8 mini mozzarella balls
8 pitted green olives
8 cherry tomatoes
4 wooden kebab sticks

Just skewer the ingredients alternately onto the kebab sticks.

Wooden kebab sticks have pointed ends and you may not want to give them to very young children.

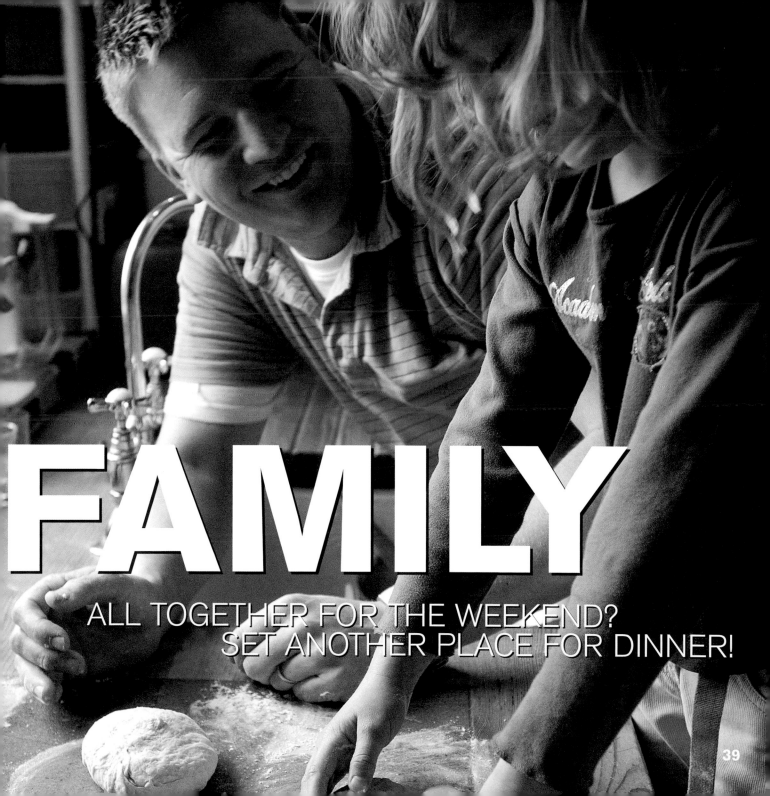

FAMILY

ALL TOGETHER FOR THE WEEKEND?
SET ANOTHER PLACE FOR DINNER!

I always think the best place for a family to get together is around the table. There's nothing like enjoying a good meal together - and maybe even helping to prepare it. Kids just love getting involved. Making bread dough or pastry is fun for everyone and helps kids appreciate the value of food.

BREAKFAST FRITTATA

MY BEST TIP FOR THIS DISH IS TO COOK THE SAUSAGES AND BACON THE NIGHT BEFORE – ESPECIALLY IF IT'S GOING TO BE A HEAVY NIGHT!

Here's how...

Drizzle a little oil over the bacon and sausages and grill until golden brown. Allow to cool, chop and set aside.

Slice the mushrooms and fry in a non-stick pan. Add the chopped bacon and sausages and keep warm.

Using a pair of scissors, cut the vine cherry tomatoes into portions and place on an oven tray. Drizzle with a little olive oil and balsamic vinegar, then sprinkle with sugar. Roast in the oven at 175°C for 10 minutes.

Meanwhile take a large mixing bowl and whisk the eggs with the milk and pepper. Add chopped chives and the sausage, bacon and mushrooms. Turn the heat up on the frying pan, add the egg mixture and fry like an omelette. Run a pallet knife round the edge of the pan to loosen the frittata.

Finally, if you have a metal handled pan place it in the oven for five minutes. If not, place the pan under a pre-heated grill for three or four minutes to cook the top.

Flip the frittata over onto a chopping board and cut into quarters. Serve with the roasted cherry tomatoes and dress with the juices from them.

Ingredients

Serves four

2 tbsps olive oil
6 rashers dry
    cured bacon
4 Cumberland
    sausages
12 button
    mushrooms
6 free range eggs
50ml milk
freshly ground
    black pepper
1 bunch chives,
    chopped

Tomatoes

4 small vines of
    cherry tomatoes
2 tbsp olive oil
1 tbsp balsamic
    vinegar
1 tsp sugar

PIZZA WITH THE KIDS

KIDS LOVE EATING PIZZAS – AND MAKING THEM, TOO. THIS RECIPE IS A GREAT WAY OF GETTING THEM TO HELP OUT IN THE FAMILY KITCHEN.

Ingredients

Makes 4 pizzas

250g strong white bread flour
250g '00' pasta flour
1 tsp salt
1 tbsp sugar
7g dried yeast
50ml olive oil
300ml warm water

10 vine tomatoes
2 cloves garlic
1 tbsp balsamic vinegar
2 tsp sugar
1 tsp salt
1 sprig thyme
4 tbsp olive oil

3 x 125g balls mozzarella
12 olives
1 large bunch basil
freshly ground black pepper

Here's how...

Place the two flours and salt in a bowl and run your hand through to get them mixed together. Make a well in the middle and add the sugar, yeast, oil and warm water.

Use your hand to stir the water and oil. As you do so the flour will start to break down into the liquid. Continue until all the flour is mixed and you have a dough-like mixture.

By now you will be in a right mess, but just keep working the dough and it will come good in the end. If your dough is crumbly, add a little water a splash at a time; likewise if your dough is really wet add a sprinkle of flour and keep on kneading.

When you have a nice smooth dough leave it in a bowl in a warm place to prove for 20 to 30 minutes until it doubles in size.

While the dough is proving you can make the tomato sauce. Cut the vine tomatoes in half and place on a baking tray with the garlic cloves. Drizzle a little balsamic vinegar over each tomato to bring out the flavour.

Continues over page

Sprinkle the tomatoes with a little sugar and salt. Rub some fresh thyme between your hands so that the leaves fall onto the tomatoes. Drizzle a good olive oil over the top – just enough to give the tomatoes a nice shine – and roast in the oven for 25 minutes at 130°C.

Take the tomatoes and garlic out of the oven, allow to cool, and pulse a few times in a food processor. Alternatively push through a sieve. Set the sauce aside.

Place the proven dough onto a floured work surface and cut into four balls of dough about the size of your fist. Press each dough ball down gently then use a rolling pin to roll out into a flat pizza shape, turning the pizza after each time you roll.

Spoon the sauce into the middle of each pizza and stir it outwards until you reach the edge. Top with mozzarella, olives, basil leaves or whatever topping takes your fancy. Season with black pepper.

Place the pizza on an oven tray or pizza stone and bake for 6 to 8 minutes as high as the oven will go, preferably 240°C

Chef's tip If you wish, any unused sauce can be frozen or kept in a sterilised jar in the fridge for later use with pasta.

PESTO AND PINE NUT LINGUINE

THIS RECIPE ORIGINATES FROM OUR FAMILY FRIENDS
FRANCESCO AND MARINA, WITH WHOM WE STAYED ON
HOLIDAY IN TUSCANY. ONCE YOU'VE TRIED IT, YOU'LL NEVER
USE SUPERMARKET PESTO AGAIN.

Here's how...

To start with there are two options – using a
food processor or a pestle and mortar to
blend the pesto.

Whichever you choose, mix the basil leaves,
sea salt and garlic with the olive oil and
smash until soft. Mix in the cheeses and pine
nuts (reserving a few to garnish) and finally
add a squeeze of lemon to balance the oil.

Place the linguine in a large pan of boiling
salted water and cook for 9 to10 minutes.

When the pasta is cooked pour it into a
colander, making sure you catch a little of
the cooking water (about two or three
tablespoons) in the saucepan.

Add the pesto to the cooking water together
with the breadcrumbs and mix together into
a creamy pesto sauce.

Finally, add the pasta and the reserved
toasted pine nuts. Stir everything together and
serve with the chopped cherry tomatoes.

Ingredients

Serves four

Pesto
2 large handfuls
    basil leaves
pinch of sea salt
3 cloves garlic
100ml olive oil
50g Parmesan cheese
50g Pecorino cheese
100g pine nuts,
    toasted
lemon juice

400g linguine
1 slice dry bread,
    whizzed to make
    breadcrumbs
12 cherry tomatoes

BAKED CAMBAZOLA CHEESE
BLUE CHEESE AND ROASTED GARLIC (MUCH MILDER THAN RAW) MAKE A PERFECT DINNER PARTY STARTER OR INDULGENT SNACK.

Here's how...
Place the bulb of garlic in some foil with a good glug of olive oil and two sprigs of rosemary, then screw the foil up into a parcel and roast in the oven for 30 minutes at 170°C. When the garlic is ready remove from the oven and leave to rest for 5 minutes. Leave the oven on for the cheese.

Meanwhile cut the garlic clove into spikes and push them into the top of the cheese. Do the same with remaining rosemary leaves and top with one or two dabs of butter. Wrap the cheese in foil so that just the top is showing.

Pour a little dry white wine over the cheese and place in the oven for 10 minutes. After five minutes warm the ciabatta alongside it in the oven until you are ready to serve.

Place everything on a chopping board and tell your guests the best way to eat this is to squeeze a roasted clove of garlic onto a slice of bread and spread it like butter. Then take a good scoop of the cheese and tuck in!

Ingredients
Serves four

1 bulb and an extra
   clove of garlic
25ml olive oil
3 sprigs rosemary
250g Cambazola
50g butter
splash of dry white
   wine
1 large loaf ciabatta
   bread

RED WINE RISOTTO WITH MONKFISH

THIS IS REAL COMFORT FOOD – AND A GREAT WAY
OF SERVING FISH WITHOUT OVERCOOKING IT.

Here's how...

Cut the monkfish up into 2cm thick slices.
Chop the onions and garlic, place in a large
pan and fry until soft with a little olive oil. Add
the rice and cook for another 2 to 3 minutes.
Add the five spice, red wine and balsamic
vinegar.

Keep on stirring the rice over a medium heat
and add the vegetable stock a ladle at a time
until it is soaked up. Taste the rice to check if
it is al dente (15 to 20 minutes) and when it
is cooked add the butter and parsley and
season with salt and pepper. Finally add the
monkfish and stir it in well.

Place a lid on the pan, remove from heat, and
go and set your dining table. While you are
doing that the fish will cook with the residual
heat.

Ingredients

Serves four

800g monkfish fillet
2 red onions
2 cloves garlic
30ml olive oil
350g risotto rice
1 tsp five spice
½ bottle red wine
3 tbsp balsamic
    vinegar
750ml vegetable stock
75g butter
1 handful flat leaf
    parsley
salt and freshly ground
    black pepper

FILLET OF SALMON WITH LEMON AND HORSERADISH GRATIN

LEMON AND HORSERADISH ARE NATURAL PARTNERS WITH TROUT OR SALMON. THE DIFFERENCE HERE IS THAT THE FLAVOURS COME FROM POTATO GRATIN SERVED ALONGSIDE.

Here's how...

Gratin Place the cream, milk, horseradish and lemon zest in a pan and bring to the boil. Then turn off and leave to cool.

Peel and slice the potatoes as thinly as you can, place them in a mixing bowl and season with plenty of salt and pepper and the chopped chives.

Arrange the potatoes in a buttered oven proof dish, ensuring that the slices lie flat. Add a squeeze of lemon juice, then pour over the infused cream, add a few knobs of butter and bake for one hour at 175°C.

Check if the potatoes are cooked by pushing a butter knife into the gratin. If it goes in without too much effort then it's cooked. Remove the gratin from the oven and leave to rest while you cook the salmon.

Salmon Season with salt and pepper and a few fennel seeds, drizzle with a little olive oil and place on a pre-heated grill pan. Cook for 5 minutes skin-side down, then 3 to 4 minutes on the other side. When the juices run white and milky, the salmon is cooked. Serve with the gratin and a dressed green salad.

Ingredients
Serves four

Gratin
250ml double cream
250ml milk
3 tbsp horseradish zest and juice of 1 lemon
4 large potatoes
salt and freshly ground black pepper
1 handful chives, chopped
50g butter

Salmon
4 x 250g salmon fillets
salt and freshly ground black pepper
fennel seeds
2 tbsp olive oil

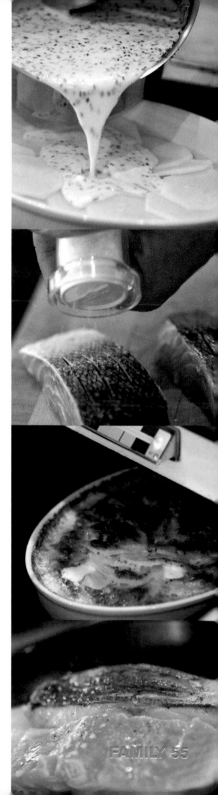

SUNDAY BEST

AN ENGLISH CLASSIC FOR THE WHOLE FAMILY –
AND ONE OF MY FAIL-SAFE FAVOURITES. GOOD
LOCAL BEEF IS THE KEY.

Here's how...

Buy a good rib of beef from your local
butcher. Season with salt, pepper and English
mustard powder and place in a large roasting
tray

Chop up two or three onions and spread
around the beef, add a generous glass of red
wine and place in the oven at 220°C for
20 minutes then turn the oven down to
180°C for 40 minutes.

Peel the potatoes and boil in salted water for
10 minutes. When they are cooked pour into
a colander and shake them about to rough up
the edges a little.

Leave the potatoes in the colander to let them
dry out. This will help you to get good, crisp
roast potatoes.

Cover the base of a large roasting tray with
olive oil about 1cm deep, add a smashed
garlic clove and a few sprigs of rosemary.

Place the roasting tray in the oven to preheat
for 10 minutes, then add the potatoes and
turn them so they will cook all over.

Ingredients

Serves four

1kg rib of beef
2 tsp salt
1 tsp pepper
4 tsp English mustard
   powder
2 or 3 onions
150ml red wine
50g butter

Roast potatoes

4 Maris Piper potatoes
1 tsp salt
50ml olive oil
1 clove garlic
2 sprigs rosemary

Yorkshire puddings

125g plain flour
200ml milk
4 eggs
50ml oil

Baby carrots

16 baby carrots
300ml water
200ml Marsala
1 tsp salt
2 tbsp sugar

Continues over page

If you have a meat thermometer, the beef needs to be 50°C for rare, 60°C for medium and 70°C for well done. When the beef is cooked cover with foil and leave to rest for 10 to 20 minutes

Meanwhile, in a bowl mix the plain flour, milk and eggs, then whisk together until smooth and leave to rest for 10 minutes.

Turn the oven up and place a Yorkshire pudding tray in the oven with about 1cm of oil in each compartment.

When the oil is smoking pour the Yorkshire pudding batter into the tray so that the compartments are full to the top. Cook for 10 to 15 minutes

Meanwhile peel and wash the carrots. Pour the water, Marsala, salt and sugar into a saucepan, bring to the boil then simmer the carrots for 10 minutes until they are tender. Check if they are done by tasting one.

For the gravy pour off the juices from the beef tray, skim off the excess oil and reduce (boil down) the gravy by half in a saucepan. Whisk in some butter, salt and pepper and serve.

Chef's Tip Instead of gravy, try a light sauce made from 1 tablespoon horseradish, 1 tablespoon wholegrain mustard, 2 tablespoons crème fraiche and salt and pepper. It goes perfectly with roast beef.

LEMON SYLLABUB

ONE OF MY ALL TIME FAVOURITES. THIS IS JUST GREAT ON AN INDIAN SUMMER'S DAY AFTER GOING BLACKBERRYING OUT ON THE FELLS.

Here's how...

Syllabub Place the blackberries in a bowl with a sprinkling of sugar and squeeze the lime over them. Zest and juice the lemons.

Whisk together the eggs and the rest of the sugar in a bowl over a pan of simmering water. Continue to whisk until the mixture doubles in size, then leave to cool.

Add the lemon juice and zest to the egg mixture, whisk the double cream to a soft peak and fold it into the egg mixture.

Spoon the blackberries into the bottom of a glass, top with the syllabub and place in the fridge to cool for an hour.

Shortbreads Place the flour, polenta, icing sugar, orange zest, hazelnuts and butter in a food processor and pulse until the mixture is a crumble consistency. If you don't have a food processor, finely chop the hazelnuts or bash them with a rolling pin and mix by hand. Add the eggs to form a dough. Roll out the dough into a 15cm long sausage and place in the fridge for 40 minutes.

Cut the dough into about 15 x 1 cm slices and place on a tray lined with baking parchment. Bake for 12 minutes at 175°C. When cooked, set aside on a wire cooling rack before serving.

Ingredients

Serves four

Syllabub

100g blackberries
100g caster sugar
1 lime
2 lemons
5 eggs
250ml double
   cream

Shortbread

225g plain flour
25g polenta
100g icing sugar
zest of 1 orange
75g hazelnuts
200g butter
2 large eggs

TIRAMISU

I LIKE TO MAKE TIRAMISU IN COFFEE CUPS AS IT IS EASY
AND LOOKS ATTRACTIVE WHEN SERVED, BUT YOU CAN
JUST AS EASILY MAKE IT IN A SINGLE LARGE BOWL.

Here's how...

Break up the muffins or cake and divide between
four cups. Add a shot of espresso and a drizzle of
brandy to each cup.

In a large mixing bowl whisk the double cream to
a soft peak so that it just starts to fall off the
spoon. Add the mascarpone and icing sugar and
mix well.

Spoon the mixture into the coffee cups and
spread flat to the rim. Dust with cocoa powder
and place in the fridge for an hour before serving.

Ingredients

Serves four

2 chocolate
    muffins,
    chocolate cake
    or Italian cake
    fingers
4 x 35ml shots of
    espresso coffee
70ml brandy
250ml double
    cream
200g mascarpone
    cheese
100g icing sugar
2 tbsp bitter cocoa
    powder

BOYS' WEEKEND

NO FRILLS. EASY TO PREPARE. THERE'S MORE TIME TO PLAY!

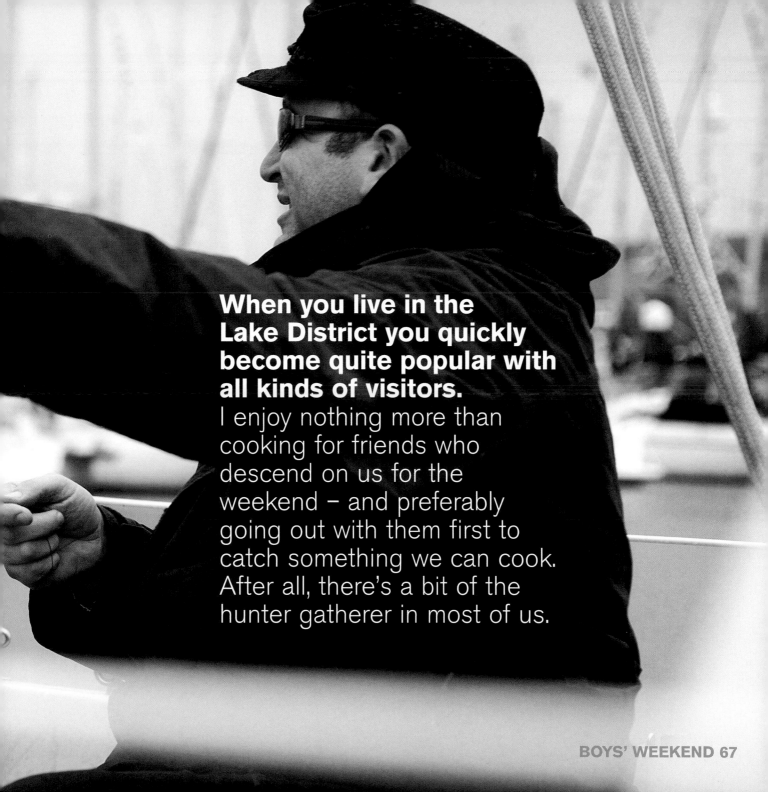

When you live in the Lake District you quickly become quite popular with all kinds of visitors. I enjoy nothing more than cooking for friends who descend on us for the weekend – and preferably going out with them first to catch something we can cook. After all, there's a bit of the hunter gatherer in most of us.

BLACK BACON BUTTIES WITH CHUTNEY

THIS BREAKFAST SANDWICH IS JUST RIGHT IF YOU'RE AIMING TO KICK-START A BUSY, FUN-FILLED WEEKEND.

Here's how...

Chutney Chop the onion and garlic and fry until soft over a medium heat. Add the tomatoes, vinegar, sugar and wine plus the remaining ingredients. Simmer for 45 minutes until jam-like. Pour into a sterilised jam jar, seal and allow to cool. Keeps in the fridge for up to one month.

Bacon Ask your butcher for a dry cured bacon joint. Once you're back home, turn it skin side down in a bowl, pour over the soy sauce and the black treacle and massage into the bacon. Turn the bacon over into the marinade and leave in a fridge overnight.

Cut the bacon joint into good thick slices and place on a hot grill pan. While the bacon is cooking slice the cherry tomatoes in half and place on the grill with the bacon.

Turn the bacon over and continue to cook for another couple of minutes. Meanwhile butter the bread for the butties and make the tea. Make your sandwiches with the bacon, tomatoes and chutney, and enjoy.

Ingredients

Serves four

Chutney

1 large onion
1 clove garlic
500g cherry tomatoes
4 tbsp white wine vinegar
3 tbsp soft brown sugar
100ml dry white wine
1 star anise
1 bay leaf
sprig of thyme
salt and freshly ground black pepper

Bacon

500g joint of bacon
4 tbsp dark soy sauce
4 tbsp black treacle
8 cherry tomatoes
50g butter
8 slices bloomer bread

SALMON BY THE LAKE

IN THE MORNING BEFORE I MEET MY FRIENDS FOR
FISHING I LIKE TO MAKE AN AROMATIC MARINADE FOR THE
SALMON – JUST IN CASE WE CATCH ONE!

Here's how...

Mix together the marinade ingredients and
sprinkle over the flesh of both pieces of
salmon.

Slice the butter and lay the slices along one
of the salmon sides. Place the other on top.

Tie the sides together with string and drizzle
with a little oil.

Heat a solid iron grill pan and cook for 20
minutes each side. Set aside to rest for a few
minutes before serving.

You can check if the salmon has cooked by
pushing a knife into one of the sides. The
flesh should have turned a nice pink if it is
ready. Alternatively, the salmon can be cooked
at home in the oven for about 30 minutes
at 180°C.

Ingredients

Serves up to eight
people

2 sides of fresh
   salmon
50g butter
30 ml olive oil

Marinade
2 tbsp smoked paprika
2 tbsp five spice
1 tbsp sugar
1 tbsp salt

PAKORA STYLE ONIONS WITH RAITA YOGHURT DIP

EVERYONE SECRETLY LOVES ONION RINGS - AND THIS RECIPE OFFERS A LIGHTER, MORE MODERN VARIATION.

Here's how...

To make the dip, add chopped mint to the yoghurt. Cut the cucumber lengthways into quarters, cut away the seeds, then chop finely and add to the yoghurt. Season with salt and pepper and it's ready to serve.

Blend the paste ingredients in a food processor or pestle and mortar. For the onion batter, place the flour in a bowl with the paste and whisk in the water and lemon juice. For best results the batter needs to be thick enough to coat the back of a spoon.

Peel the onions and slice into rings about 1cm thick. Place the onions into a pan of boiling water for one minute, then transfer to cold water. Drain thoroughly.

Fill a saucepan a third full of oil and heat. Drain the onions and toss them in flour before dipping them in the batter. Slide the onion rings into the hot oil, cooking only 3 or 4 at a time.

The cooked onion rings can be placed on a wire rack in the oven on low heat to keep them warm while you fry the rest.

Ingredients

Serves four

Dip

1 large handful fresh mint
200ml Greek yoghurt
1 cucumber
salt and freshly ground black pepper

Paste

1 tsp ground cumin
1 tsp ground coriander
2 tsp garam masala
1 tsp chilli powder
1 tsp salt
1 tsp turmeric
1 tsp tomato puree
3 cloves garlic, crushed
1 thumb of fresh ginger

400g flour
500ml soda or sparkling mineral water
juice of ½ lemon
4 large white onions
vegetable oil

BOYS' WEEKEND 73

ROAST PUMPKIN HUMMUS WITH HOME-MADE FLAT BREADS

THIS RECIPE WAS SUGGESTED BY ONE OF MY TALENTED CHEFS WHO PICKED UP THE IDEA BACK HOME IN NEW ZEALAND.

Here's how...

Cut the pumpkin into quarters and scoop out the seeds. Score a criss-cross into the flesh with a knife. Season with salt, pepper, cumin and a drizzle of olive oil. Place the pumpkin in the oven for 40 minutes at about 180°C .

When the pumpkin has cooled scrape out the cooked flesh with a spoon and place in a food processor (use a hand-held blender if you do not have a food processor). Add the garlic, half of the chick peas and lemon juice and blend. Pour in the olive oil until the mix becomes a smooth paste.

Season to taste with salt, pepper and more garlic if desired. Add more lemon juice if it needs sharpening up.

Add the remaining chick peas and pulse the food processor a couple of times. This gives the hummus a bit of texture so it's not just baby food.

Serve the hummus with a few pumpkin seeds and a final drizzle of olive oil. If you want a little kick, a bit of chilli oil would be good - just to let you know it's there!

Serve with pitta bread or use my focaccia bread recipe (page 31) and roll out into pitta-shaped flat breads. Bake at 220°C for 10 minutes or so.

Ingredients

Serves four

½ medium pumpkin
   or 1 butternut
   squash
salt and freshly
   ground black
   pepper
1 tbsp cumin
75ml olive oil, plus
   extra for drizzling
2 large cloves garlic
300g chick peas,
   cooked or tinned
juice of 2 lemons
pumpkin seeds,
   to serve

WEST COAST MACKEREL AND LEMON CROSTINI

MACKEREL IS AN UNDERRATED FISH, BUT IT REALLY COMES INTO ITS OWN WITH THIS SIMPLE RECIPE.

Here's how...

Cut the baguette into long slices and rub all over with one half of a garlic clove. Pour half the olive oil over the baguette slices and bake in the oven for 15 minutes at 180°C.

Turn the mackerel fillets so they are skin side up, cut them in half and make small cuts in the skin about every centimetre or so.

Season well, making sure you work the salt and pepper into the cuts. Coat the fish in flour and set aside. Do not do this too early or the flour will soak into the fish and spoil the taste.

Heat a frying pan until it is just starting to smoke. Drizzle the remaining oil over the fillets on the skin side and place them in the pan skin side down. As they are cooking press them down to stop them from curling and burning on the sides.

After one minute or so flip them over and squeeze half the lemon juice all over the fish. Remove from the heat.

Chop the capers and parsley and mix in a bowl with the mayonnaise and remaining lemon juice. Spoon a portion onto each of the baguette slices and top with a mackerel fillet.

Ingredients

Serves four

1 baguette sliced
1 clove garlic
3 tbsp olive oil
4 fillets of mackerel
salt and freshly
    ground black
    pepper
50g flour
juice of 1 lemon
100g capers
handful of flat leaf
    parsley
4 tbsp mayonnaise

MOROCCAN ROAST LAMB

I'M A HUGE FAN OF MEDITERRANEAN FOOD - AND HERE I'VE COMBINED OUR LOCAL LAMB WITH SOME OF THE GREAT FLAVOURS OF NORTH AFRICA.

Here's how...

Ask your butcher for a good quality local leg of lamb. Place the lamb in a large roasting tray and use a pointed knife to make several cuts in the meat until you hit the bone. This makes small pockets that let the marinade penetrate to the centre of the lamb.

Peel and chop the garlic and place in a bowl with the cumin, olive oil, turmeric and mint. Lastly add the zest and juice of the lemon.

Mix the marinade together, pour it over the lamb and massage it into the meat. Take your time as the more you work at it, the more flavour will get into the dish. Leave the lamb for one hour to absorb the flavour.

Place the lamb in the oven at 200°C for 30 minutes and then turn down to 150°C for a further hour.

The dishes that follow can be cooked while the lamb is roasting and left to serve at room temperature. Couscous and aubergines (next page) make a perfect combination with roast lamb.

Ingredients

Serves four to six

2kg leg of lamb, on the bone
4 cloves garlic
4 tbsp cumin
50ml olive oil
1 tbsp turmeric
4 tbsp dried mint
1 lemon

ROASTED LEMON AND MINT COUSCOUS

Here's how...

For the couscous, place a large saucepan on the heat and add enough olive oil to cover the bottom of the pan.

Chop the onion and garlic finely and fry for two to three minutes until they soften. Add the cumin and couscous and stir so that all the couscous is coated in the oil. Add the vegetable stock and stir well. Bring to the boil and then turn off the heat. Place a lid on the pan and leave for 15 minutes to let the couscous absorb the liquid.

Meanwhile place a frying pan on the heat. Cut your lemons in half and rub the cut surface with a little olive oil. Place the lemons cut side down in the pan and leave on a low heat to caramelise. It will take about 10 minutes for them to go a lovely golden brown. When the lemons are cooked remove from the heat and leave to cool slightly so you can handle them.

Using a fork stir up the couscous until it is loose and fluffy. Squeeze the lemons into the couscous followed by a generous glug of extra virgin olive oil. Finish the dish with lots of freshly chopped mint and a handful of toasted pine nuts plus salt and pepper to taste.

Ingredients

Serves four

3 tbsp olive oil
1 white onion
1 garlic clove
1 tbsp cumin
300g couscous
500ml vegetable
  stock
2 lemons
extra virgin olive oil
1 large bunch of
  fresh mint
50g pine nuts,
  toasted
salt and freshly
  ground black
  pepper

GRILLED AUBERGINES

Here's how...

Place a grill pan on the heat to get smoking hot. Slice the aubergines at a 45° angle about ½ cm thick. Put the sliced aubergines in a bowl, pour over a little olive oil and season with salt and pepper. Use your hands to turn over the aubergines so that they are coated in the oil and seasoning.

Cover the grill pan with slices of aubergine and cook for a minute or so. Turn them over and cook for a further minute before removing and placing them in another bowl. Repeat the process until you have cooked all the aubergine slices.

To dress the aubergines, add the zest and juice of one lemon and the remaining olive oil. Use a fine grater to grate in the garlic and chilli. Stop grating the chilli when you get to the seeds (unless you want it really hot). Finish the dish with freshly chopped mint and serve.

Ingredients

Serves four

2 aubergines
50 ml olive oil
salt and freshly ground
    black pepper
1 lemon
½ clove garlic
1 chilli
1 handful mint

THAI BUTTERNUT SQUASH CURRY

THIS LIGHT AND FRAGRANT CURRY
COMBINES PERFECTLY WITH THE
SWEETNESS OF BUTTERNUT SQUASH.

Here's how...

Place the paste ingredients into a food processor or pestle and mortar and blend. Save a few selected coriander leaves for use as garnish.

Slice the red onions and the peppers. Peel and dice the butternut squash into 1cm cubes.

Heat a wok with a little vegetable oil. When it is hot add the butternut squash and cook for four to five minutes, then add the peppers, green beans and onions. Add 4 tablespoons of the paste and stir in well. Finally add the coconut cream and simmer gently for 10 minutes or so.

To check if the curry is ready taste a piece of the butternut squash, which takes the longest to cook. To finish the dish add plenty of freshly chopped coriander and toasted cashew nuts.

To cook the rice measure out four handfuls and place in a pan with one litre of water. Bring to the boil, cover and simmer for 20 minutes or so until cooked. Check if it is al dente by tasting some rice on a fork.

Chef's tip When the rice is cooked pour it into a colander and rinse with a kettle full of boiling water. This washes away a lot of the starch and makes for better rice.

Ingredients
Serves four to six

Paste
4 medium green chillies, de-seeded and roughly chopped
2 shallots, roughly chopped
1 thumb of fresh ginger, peeled and grated
2 garlic cloves
small bunch of fresh coriander, stalks and roots attached if possible
2 lemon grass stalks
zest and juice of 1 lime
8 kaffir lime leaves, torn into pieces (if unavailable, use the grated zest of 1 extra lime)
2 tsp Thai fish sauce or (for vegetarians) light soy sauce
3 tbsp ground nut oil

Curry and rice
2 red onions
2 red peppers
2 butternut squashes
vegetable oil
100g green beans
1 tin of coconut cream
handful fresh coriander, chopped
100g cashew nuts, toasted
4 handfuls jasmine rice

CHORIZO AND RIOJA
A PERFECT TV SNACK. IT MAY NOT BE EASY TO
PRONOUNCE – BUT BOY, IS IT GOOD TO EAT!

Here's how...
Preheat the oven to 180°C. Dice the
chorizo into 1cm chunks and place in an
ovenproof dish with the wine and (if you
like it hot) the chilli. Leave the chorizo to
cook in the oven for 30 minutes.

Serve with a crusty loaf, Serrano ham,
olives and some roasted almonds – or
just tuck in without any trimmings except
your favourite bread!

Ingredients
Serves four to six

300g chorizo sausage
½ bottle Rioja red wine
½ red chilli

ROASTED PINEAPPLE AND MALIBU ICE CREAM

DON'T LET ANYONE TELL YOU THAT REAL MEN DON'T
LIKE PUDS. THIS ONE'S A SURE FIRE HIT!

Here's how...

For this recipe you can cheat a little to save time – start by buying a good quality vanilla ice cream.

Place the ice cream in a mixer and soften on a low speed. Add the Malibu a little at a time. The best way to get this right is to taste it. I know I say this all the time – but the fact is that my taste might be different from yours.

When you have added enough liqueur, return the ice cream to the original container and place it back in the freezer. No-one need ever know!

Take the pineapple and cut off the top and the bottom. Then cut off the peel downwards round the pineapple so that all you have left is the fruit.

Heat a grill pan. Cut the pineapple into six to eight lengthways and remove the central core which can be a bit tough. Then halve the slices again across the middle.

Sprinkle the pineapple with caster sugar and place on a hot griddle pan until you get those gorgeous char-grilled markings. Remember you are not really cooking the pineapple, you are just creating a scorched, caramelised flavour.

When you have got a good colour on them, remove the pineapple segments from the pan and serve with the ice cream and a drizzle of Malibu.

Ingredients

Serves four

500ml tub vanilla
    ice cream
100ml Malibu
1 fresh ripened
    pineapple
50g caster sugar

CAFÉ
TAKE A BREAK. JUST RELAX.
A FEW MINUTES FOR YOURSELF!

**A café is all about people –
staff and customers.**
My *Good Taste* café in Keswick
sees the same regulars
dropping in at the same time
every day. Maybe people are
moving towards a continental
café culture. We go for
simplicity, quality and freshness
– and our customers pick up on
our passion for good food.

CAFÉ

GREEK YOGHURT BREAKFAST POT

A HEALTHY AND TASTY START TO THE DAY –
BUT YOU WILL HAVE TO PREPARE THE
COMPOTE THE DAY BEFORE.

Here's how...

Quarter the plums and remove the stones.
Place the star anise, cinnamon stick, sugar
and orange juice in a saucepan and dissolve
the sugar on a low heat for about 10 minutes.

Add the plums and continue to cook for about
15 minutes. Try not to use a spoon to stir, just
shake the pan gently otherwise you will break
up the plums. When they are cooked but still
intact remove from the heat and place in a
clean jar. Refrigerate.

The compote will keep for several days in the
fridge. Alternatively you can use fresh berries
or even a tablespoon of your favourite jam.

To serve, spoon some of the plum compote
into the bottom of a glass and add Greek
yoghurt. Grate the lime zest over the yoghurt
and add a squeeze of lime juice if you wish.
Finally top the dish with muesli and serve.

Ingredients

Serves four

500g plums
1 star anise
1 cinnamon stick
200g sugar
75 ml orange juice
500g Greek yoghurt
zest and juice of 1 lime
250g good qualily
    muesli

POACHED EGGS WITH TOASTED MUFFINS AND CARAMELISED PANCETTA

HERE'S A LIGHT AND EASY VARIATION ON THE CLASSIC EGG AND BACON THEME.

Here's how...

Grill the pancetta until it is crisp, then brush with a little honey or dust with icing sugar. Place in the top oven to keep warm.

To poach the eggs, bring a saucepan of salted water to the boil and add the vinegar. Reduce the heat until the water is just bubbling and stir with a spoon to create a whirlpool motion.

Crack the eggs into a small bowl so that you can slide them into the water rather than dropping them in.

Cook for three minutes, then remove the poached eggs with a slotted spoon.

To serve, butter the toasted muffins and top with the pancetta and poached eggs. Mill a little black pepper on top and serve.

Ingredients

Serves four

8 rashers pancetta
   or streaky bacon
2 tsp honey or
   icing sugar
2 tbsp vinegar
8 free range local eggs
butter
4 muffins, toasted
freshly ground black
   pepper

TOASTED MUESLI BREAD
WITH BLUEBERRY JAM

MUESLI MAKES A REALLY HEALTHY BREAD THAT
IS JUST RIGHT FOR BREAKFAST TOAST.

Here's how...

Jam Place the blueberries in a thick bottomed pan with the lime zest and juice, simmer for 10 minutes, add the sugar and stir until dissolved. Bring to the boil and continue to cook for 25 minutes or so. Remove from the heat and skim off any impurities and scum. Leave the jam to set for 20 minutes or so then pour into sterilised jam jars and seal.

Bread Roast the hazelnuts on a baking tray in the oven for 10 minutes at 180°C.

Place the two flours, yeast, sugar and salt in a bowl and mix, making a well in the centre. Pour in the water and olive oil. Using your hands, mix together until the dough comes away from the bowl, then transfer to a floured surface. Continue to knead until the dough is smooth, then add the muesli and the hazelnuts. Knead for another minute or two.

Leave the dough in a bowl in a warm place to prove for 20 to 30 minutes until it doubles in size.

Cut the dough into two equal portions and shape into 500g (1lb) non-stick loaf tins. Leave the loaves somewhere warm to prove and double in size (about 20 minutes).

Brush the tops of the bread with beaten egg to give them a golden colour, then bake in a hot oven for about 30 minutes at 200°C.

To check if the loaves are cooked remove them from the tins and tap the underside. If it sounds hollow the loaves are ready. Serve sliced and toasted, with blueberry jam.

Ingredients

Makes two loaves

Jam
500g blueberries
zest and juice of 2 limes
450g preserving sugar

Bread
50g hazelnuts
100g rye flour
400g strong white
   bread flour
7g dried yeast
2 tbsp sugar
1 tbsp salt
300ml warm water
25ml vegetable oil
100g muesli with
   dried fruit
1 egg, beaten, to glaze

SCONES

SCONES ARE ALL ABOUT TOUCH AND FEEL.
THEY NEED TO BE FIRM WHEN THEY GO INTO
THE OVEN SO THAT THEY WILL RISE PROPERLY
AND NOT SPREAD OUTWARDS.

Here's how...

Soak your flavour ingredients – in this case the
sultanas – in 300ml warm water with the saffron
for 5 minutes.

Sieve the flour and baking powder into a bowl.
Rub in the butter with your fingertips to create
breadcrumbs and add the sugar. Drain the
sultanas and add to the mix.

Finally add the milk a little at a time, using a
spoon to fold the mixture together. Don't beat it,
be gentle!

Transfer the scone mixture to a floured surface
and press or roll out to about 3 cm thick. Cut out
the scones with a pastry cutter and transfer to a
non-stick baking tray. Brush with egg yolk and
bake in the oven at 200°C for 15 minutes

Chef's Tip

As alternatives to the sultanas, try blueberries
and lemon zest or apple (peeled and grated) with
ground cinnamon.

For savoury scones, try cheese and spring onions
with salt, pepper and a pinch of mustard powder.

Ingredients

Serves six

125g sultanas
pinch of saffron
   (optional)
500g self raising
   flour
25g baking powder
125g butter
100g sugar
   (if making sweet
   scones)
200ml milk
1 egg yolk, beaten,
   to glaze

CAFÉ 99

HALLOUMI AND SPINACH TART

A TASTY FUSION OF FRENCH QUICHE AND FLAVOURS OF THE EASTERN MEDITERRANEAN.

Here's how...

For the pastry, place the flour in a bowl and rub in the butter. Add one egg at a time to bind the mixture. When you have a good pastry dough, wrap in cling film and leave to rest in the fridge for 30 minutes or so.

Place the spinach in a hot pan to wilt for 2–3 minutes – just enough so that you can squeeze the water out of the spinach through a sieve.

Roll out the pastry to about 3mm thick and use to line a loose bottomed non-stick flan tin.

Squeeze out the very last drops of water from the spinach and spread out in the bottom of the pastry case. Break up the Feta cheese with your hands straight into the tin, then grate in the halloumi and sprinkle with toasted pine nuts.

Whisk together the eggs, double cream and pepper. Pour as much of the mixture into the pastry case as you can, and leave it to settle for a minute or two so it soaks into all the gaps in the tart. Top it up a little more and repeat until you've added all the cream mixture. Bake for 30 minutes at 180°C.

Ingredients

Serves six

Pastry
500g flour
250g butter
3 eggs

Filling
1 bag baby spinach
100g Feta cheese
100g halloumi
50g pine nuts, toasted
3 eggs
300ml double cream
freshly ground black
    pepper

POSH FISH FINGER SANDWICH

THESE FISH FINGERS ARE A GREAT WAY TO GET KIDS
EATING FRESH FISH WITHOUT A FIGHT.

Here's how...

Tartare sauce Place the mayonnaise in a bowl
with the capers, lemon juice and chopped parsley.
Mix well, preferably using a stick blender.

Fish Fingers Blitz the bread in a food processor
with the rosemary and lemon zest until you have
breadcrumbs.

Cut the salmon into finger-sized slices. Take three
bowls – one with the plain flour, one containing
the eggs whisked together with the milk, and one
with the breadcrumbs.

Dip the salmon into the flour and then into the
egg mixture. Change hands and transfer the
salmon from the egg mixture into the bread
crumbs. Shake the bowl so the fish is evenly
coated.

Drizzle some vegetable oil on to a baking tray and
place the fish on the tray. Top with a little more oil
– just enough to coat the fish. Bake in the oven
for 12 minutes at 180°C.

Cut the bloomer bread and spread each slice with
a generous serving of tartare sauce. Add some
shredded lettuce and the fish fingers.

Finally squeeze lemon juice over the sandwich
and top with another slice of bloomer bread.

Ingredients

Serves four

Tartare sauce

6 tbsp mayonnaise
1 tbsp capers
juice of 1 lemon
2 tbsp flat leaf
  parsley, chopped

Fish fingers

300g sliced bread
1 sprig rosemary
zest of 1 lemon
450g fresh salmon
100g flour
2 eggs
50ml milk
3 tbsp vegetable oil
8 slices traditional
  English bloomer
  bread
2 Baby Gem
  lettuces
juice of ½ lemon

BUTTERNUT SQUASH SOUP WITH ROASTED ONION FOCACCIA

A HEARTY WARMER FOR A COLD DAY – AND ONE THAT'S ESPECIALLY POPULAR WITH HILL WALKERS CALLING IN AT MY CAFÉ.

Here's how...

Peel the butternut squash, remove the seeds, dice and sauté in the oil with the onion, garlic and cumin for 3–4 minutes. Add the vegetable stock and simmer for 10–12 minutes until the squash are tender.

Blend the soup with the double cream. Season if needed and serve with a dollop of crème fraîche and a little white truffle oil.

Onion focaccia For the focaccia, chop the onion finely into slices, coat in the olive oil and roast in the oven for 35 minutes at 150°C until golden and sweet.

To make the focaccia dough, follow the recipe on page 31. Once the dough has proved, roll it out into a rectangle and spread with the roasted onions, including all the oil and juices. Top with sea salt and freshly picked rosemary.

Leave to prove for a further 15 minutes or so and then bake for 20 minutes at 180°C.

Ingredients

Serves four

Soup

2 butternut squash
2 tbsp olive oil
1 onion
2 cloves garlic
1 tsp ground cumin
600ml vegetable stock
150ml double cream
salt and freshly ground
    black pepper
3 tbsp crème fraîche,
    to serve
white truffle oil,
    to serve

Onion focaccia

Ingredients on page 31
plus:
1 large white onion
75ml olive oil
sea salt
2 sprigs rosemary

SALADS

BALSAMIC VINE TOMATOES, MOZZARELLA AND BASIL

THIS DISH IS ALL ABOUT THE QUALITY OF THE RAW INGREDIENTS, SO DON'T SKIMP. USE GOOD VINE TOMATOES IN THE SUMMER AND PLEASE, PLEASE BUY GOOD QUALITY MOZZARELLA – PREFERABLY WITH THE *BUFALA CAMPANA* LOGO.

Here's how...

Slice the tomatoes in half. Mix 30ml balsamic vinegar and the sugar in a shallow pan on a low heat.

When the sugar has dissolved, add the tomatoes and cook for two minutes or so to allow the balsamic to soak into them.

Layer up the mozzarella, tomatoes and basil as shown. Top with the toasted pine nuts and olive oil.

Finish with the remaining balsamic vinegar and season with salt and pepper.

Now turn the page for three more of our favourite salads.

Ingredients

Serves four to six

4 vine tomatoes
50ml balsamic vinegar
30g sugar
2 balls buffalo mozzarella, sliced
1 large bunch basil
2 tbsp pine nuts, toasted
30ml olive oil
salt and freshly ground black pepper

Mango and red pepper

Pear, walnut and pecorino cheese

Chorizo and new potatoes

CAFÉ 107

SALADS

MANGO AND RED PEPPER

Here's how...
Peel the mangoes and slice. Chop the red onion, red peppers and chilli and mix with the mango.

Add the white wine vinegar and olive oil.

Finish with the chopped coriander, mustard cress and a squeeze of lime juice.

Ingredients
Serves four to six

2 ripe mangoes
1 red onion
2 red peppers
1 red chilli
2 tbsp white wine
  vinegar
50ml olive oil
1 large bunch coriander
1 punnet mustard cress
juice of 1 lime

PEAR, WALNUT AND PECORINO CHEESE

Here's how...

Place the walnuts on an oven tray and roast for 10 minutes at 180°C until crisp.

Core and slice the pears and place in a large salad bowl. Pour over the lemon juice. Add the walnut oil and toss the pears, ensuring they are well covered with the dressing to stop them going brown.

Add the watercress, roasted walnuts and a little salt and pepper. Stir well so that all the pear salad is dressed. Finally, use a potato peeler to scatter Pecorino shavings over the top.

Ingredients

Serves four to six

100g walnuts
4 pears
juice of 1 lemon
50ml walnut oil
100g watercress
salt and freshly ground
   black pepper
50g medium-aged
   Pecorino cheese

CHORIZO AND NEW POTATOES

Here's how...

Cut the potatoes at an angle from one end to the other and cook in boiling salted water. To check if they're done, push a knife into a potato – if it goes in easily they're cooked.

Meanwhile dice the chorizo and place in a frying pan on a low heat. As the heat rises the fat from the chorizo will melt and come out into the pan. Use this to dress the salad.

Drain the potatoes and leave them to cool for about 5 minutes, then transfer to the frying pan with the chorizo.

Stir the pan, making sure all the potatoes are coated in the smoked chorizo oil. To finish mix in the olive oil, salt and pepper and lots of freshly chopped coriander.

Ingredients

Serves four to six

1kg new potatoes
250g chorizo sausage
100ml olive oil
salt and freshly ground
   black pepper
fresh coriander

BLUEBERRY AND PASSION FRUIT CAKE

THIS WAS ONE OF THE FIRST RECIPES I TRIED WHEN MY CAFÉ OPENED AND IT'S BEEN A FAVOURITE WITH MY REGULARS EVER SINCE.

Here's how...

Preheat the oven to 180°C. Melt a knob of butter in a pan and use it to brush two medium-sized loaf tins. Line the bottom of each tin with a piece of greaseproof paper.

In a large bowl, cream together the butter and sugar until pale and creamy, using an electric whisk or a wooden spoon. Beat well for two minutes or so to get lots of air into the mixture.

Beat in the eggs one at a time. Add a tablespoon of flour if the mixture curdles. Fold in the flour and blueberries using a large metal spoon. Be careful not to over-mix it.

Pour the mixture equally between the two cake tins and level off the top with a spatula. Make a slight dip in the centre with the tip of the spatula if you don't want them to be pointed in the middle.

Place in the oven and bake for about 30 minutes, or until the cakes spring back when pressed gently with a finger and are pale golden in colour.

Remove from the oven and take them out of the tins after about 5 to 10 minutes. Place them on a wire rack for about half an hour to cool completely.

To make the icing, cut the passion fruits in half and scrape out the pulp into a sieve. Push the fruit through the sieve to produce a clear orange-coloured juice.

Add the icing sugar and mix well to form a thick icing – it will run straight off your spoon if it is too thin.

Ice the two cakes and allow the icing to set before serving.

Ingredients

Serves eight

200g butter, plus
    extra for
    greasing
200g caster sugar
4 eggs
200g self-raising
    flour
2 handfuls of
    blueberries
3 passion fruits
150g icing sugar

SABLÉS

THESE SHORTBREADS HAVE BEEN ON THE CAFÉ MENU EVER SINCE I DISCOVERED THE RECIPE ON HOLIDAY IN FRANCE. HERE I'VE SUGGESTED A CHOCOLATE AND ORANGE VERSION – AND ANOTHER WITH LEMON AND PINE NUTS.

Here's how...

Place the butter, icing sugar and egg yolks in a mixing bowl and beat until light and fluffy.

Add the vanilla extract and orange or lemon zest and mix together.

Sieve in the flour and add the chocolate buttons or pine nuts. Mix until the dough comes together.

Place on a floured surface and shape into a 20cm long Toblerone-like triangle.

Refrigerate until firm.

Slice into 2cm thick slices and bake on a non-stick baking tray for 12 minutes at 150°C until golden.

Ingredients

Makes six to eight

Chocolate and orange sablés
250g butter (at
    room temperature)
125g icing sugar
2 medium egg yolks
1 tbsp vanilla extract
zest of 2 oranges
375g plain flour
100g dark chocolate
    buttons

Lemon and pine nut sablés
Replace the orange
    zest and chocolate
    with...
zest of 2 lemons
100g toasted
    pine nuts

BBQ

SUN'S OUT. CALL YOUR FRIENDS.
FIRE UP THE BARBIE!

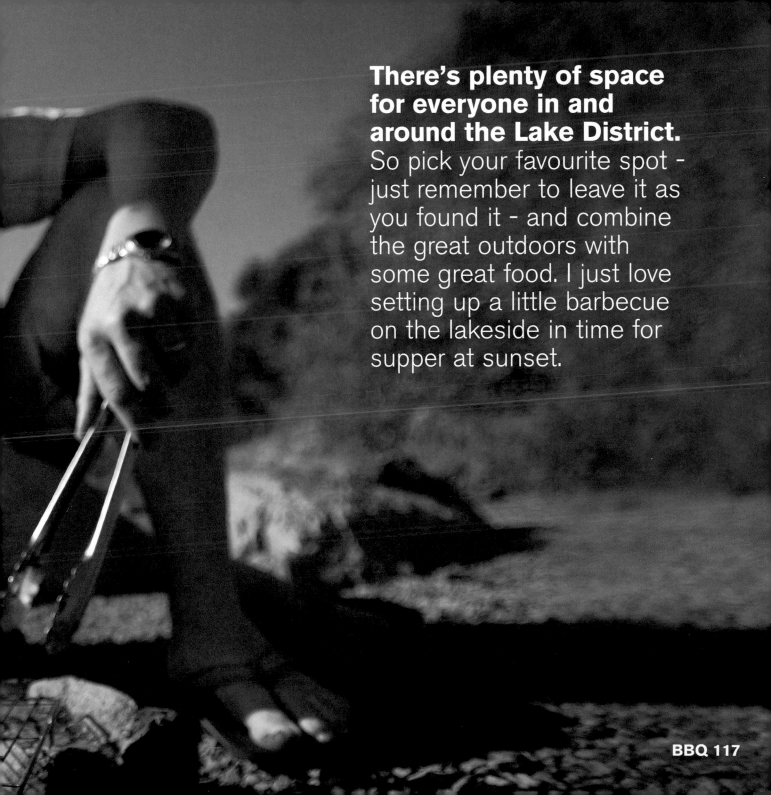

There's plenty of space for everyone in and around the Lake District. So pick your favourite spot – just remember to leave it as you found it – and combine the great outdoors with some great food. I just love setting up a little barbecue on the lakeside in time for supper at sunset.

SEA BASS WITH FENNEL AND PERNOD

THE IDEA FOR THE FENNEL BERRIES IN THIS
RECIPE CAME TO ME IN A FRIEND'S GARDEN
IN LATE SUMMER. I JUST GRABBED SOME AND
TRIED THEM – AND THERE WAS AN EXPLOSION
OF ANISEED FLAVOUR!

Here's how...

Chop the roots off the fennel bulbs and shred
the rest of the bulbs as thinly as possible.

Score each side of the sea bass six times –
this lets the flavour permeate the fish. Season
with sea salt, black pepper and the fennel
berries, making sure the seasoning is rubbed
into the cuts.

Roll out 1m of tin foil, then fold it over again
so it is double strength. Spread half the fennel
on to the foil and lay the fish on top. Stuff
lemon slices and the remaining fennel into the
fish, then drizzle it with olive oil, Pernod and
the juice from the lemon.

Wrap the foil over the fish, place it on the
barbecue and, if you have a lid, cover it so it
cooks more quickly. The sea bass should take
20–25 minutes to cook.

Ingredients

Serves four

2 fennel bulbs
1 whole sea bass
 (350–500g)
sea salt
freshly ground
 black pepper
handful of fennel
 berries (if not
 available use dried
 fennel seeds)
1 lemon
30ml olive oil
40ml Pernod or
 pastis

CAMEMBERT AND CRANBERRIES

DON'T WORRY ABOUT GETTING YOUR FINGERS
STICKY WITH THIS ONE – IT'S WORTH IT!

Here's how...

The night before your barbecue, place the dried
cranberries in a bowl with the port and leave
to soak. Next day, remove the cranberries and
drain – but don't throw away the port as it will be
used later.

Unwrap a Camembert and push cranberries
into the top, through the skin (six to eight per
cheese should do).

Place a good sprig of rosemary in the centre of a
piece of foil, about 30cm square, brush with the
butter and place the Camembert on top, lifting up
the edge to form a jacket around the cheese.

Spoon a little more port over the top of the
cheese so that it can seep into the holes created
by the cranberries.

Finally bring the corners of the foil together at the
top and pinch together to form a type of handle.
Repeat for the second Camembert.

Place the cheeses in the corners of the
barbecue, where it is not too hot, and cook for
about 10 minutes until the cheese is soft in
the middle. Serve with crostini or stuff into a
pitta bread.

Ingredients

Serves four

1 handful of dried
    cranberries
1 glass of port
2 Camembert
    cheeses
large sprig of
    rosemary
20g butter, softened

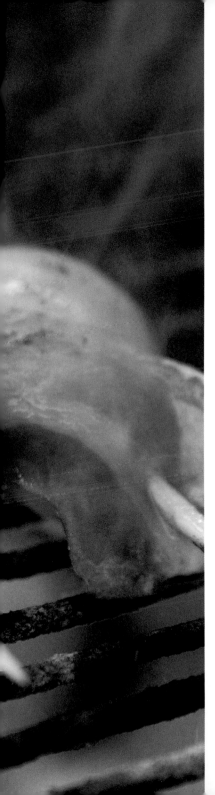

NEW POTATO, GARLIC AND PANCETTA KEBABS

THIS IDEA OF MINE IS DESIGNED TO MAKE IT EASIER –
AND TASTIER – TO BARBECUE POTATOES.

Here's how...

Before the barbecue, place the garlic bulbs in an ovenproof dish, pour a little olive oil over them and roast in the oven at 170°C for about 30 minutes until soft.

Soak the kebab sticks in water for 10 minutes or so to help prevent burning.

Cut the new potatoes in half lengthways and boil in salted water for 10 minutes. Drain and leave to cool.

When the garlic has cooled, take the cloves out of their skins, trying to keep them whole. To assemble the kebabs, thread half a potato onto one end of the stick, then slide on a garlic clove, repeating the process twice for each portion. Sprinkle rosemary over the kebabs and season with black pepper.

Take a rasher of pancetta, pierce one end with the kebab stick and wrap it like a jacket around the potatoes and garlic and fix to the other end of the stick.

Barbecue until the pancetta is cooked and serve.

Ingredients

Serves six

2 whole garlic bulbs
2 tbsp olive oil
6 wooden kebab sticks
500g new potatoes
    (cooked al dente)
freshly chopped
    rosemary
freshly ground
    black pepper
12 rashers of pancetta
    or streaky bacon

LAKELAND BURGER

WE ALL KNOW KIDS LOVE BURGERS, SO
HERE'S ONE THAT USES LOCAL INGREDIENTS
WITH A GREEK TWIST.

Here's how...

Place the mince in a bowl,
adding the peeled and
chopped garlic and anchovies.
Season with dried oregano
and black pepper, mix together
vigorously and shape into four
burgers.

Leave to rest for an hour in the
fridge, then grill each side
evenly on the barbecue.

Serve in a warm ciabatta roll
with sliced tomato and red
onion, Feta cheese, spinach
leaves and a splash of Greek
yoghurt.

Ingredients
Serves four

500g minced
    Lakeland lamb
2 garlic cloves
2 anchovies, finely
    chopped
I tbsp dried oregano
freshly ground
    black pepper
4 ciabatta rolls
3 vine tomatoes
1 red onion
100g Feta cheese
2 handfuls baby
    spinach leaves
4 tbsp Greek yoghurt

STICKY CHINESE PORK WITH CHARGRILLED SPRING ONIONS

NOT MANY CHINESE-STYLE DISHES TRANSFER EASILY
TO THE BARBECUE, BUT THIS ONE CERTAINLY DOES.

Here's how...

Chop the pork fillet into 2cm cubes and place
in a bowl. Peel and chop the garlic and ginger
finely and add to the pork. Pour over the soy
sauce, honey, sesame oil and Chinese 5 spice.
Mix until all the meat is covered and leave to
marinade for 20 minutes.

Soak the kebab sticks in water for 10 minutes
or so to help prevent burning.

Skewer the pork onto kebab sticks, about four
pieces per portion, and place them on the grill,
ensuring you cook them evenly. Using a pastry
brush, periodically baste the pork with the
remaining marinade.

While the pork is cooking, cut the roots off
the spring onions and peel away the outer
skin. Coat them in a little sesame oil and
place on the barbecue. (Alternatively you can
thread them on to the kebabs, between the
pieces of pork, as shown.)

The spring onions will need only 2–3 minutes
before they are wilted and ready to eat.

Ingredients

Serves four

400g pork fillet
3 garlic cloves
1 thumb of ginger
4 tbsp soy sauce
4 tbsp honey
20ml sesame oil, plus
    extra for coating
2 tsp Chinese 5 spice
4 kebab sticks
8 spring onions

PORCHETTA

I CAME ACROSS THIS RECIPE IN A SMALL MARKET TOWN IN TUSCANY. IT'S CLASSIC ITALIAN STREET FOOD – AND I THOUGHT, WHAT A GREAT DISH TO BRING BACK HOME!

Here's how...

Score the fat of the belly pork with a sharp knife and place in a large roasting tray. In a food processor, or using a hand-held blender, pulse the fennel, rosemary, garlic, lemon zest and juice and olive oil.

Pour the marinade over the pork, rubbing it all over to make sure it gets into the cuts in the fat. Season the pork with plenty of sea salt and freshly ground black pepper.

Either cook on a spit for 2–3 hours, turning continually with a beer in your other hand, or roast in the oven for 1½ hours at 180°C.

Serving suggestion Try this one with a dressed salad of cherry tomatoes, gnocchi and baby spinach.

Ingredients

Serves four to six

1 kilo belly pork, boned
2 fennel bulbs, roughly
   chopped
4 large sprigs of
   rosemary
6 cloves garlic
zest and juice of
   1 lemon
50ml olive oil
4 tbsp sea salt
freshly ground
   black pepper

BAKED SWEET POTATOES WITH CHILLI AND CUMIN BUTTER

HERE'S ANOTHER TASTIER ALTERNATIVE TO BAKED POTATOES.

Here's how...

Wash and wrap the sweet potatoes in foil and cook on a low heat area of the barbecue for about 1 hour until soft.

For the butter, toast the cumin and coriander seeds gently in a pan until they start to pop. Remove them and crush with a pestle and mortar.

Deseed and chop the chillies. Combine with the cumin and coriander and the softened butter. Finally mix in the chopped coriander and leave to cool.

Cut a cross into the sweet potatoes, add a spoonful of the butter mixture and serve.

This recipe also works well if the potatoes are baked in the oven for 30 minutes or so at 180°C.

Ingredients

Serves four

4 large sweet potatoes
1 tbsp cumin seeds
1 tbsp coriander seeds
2 red chillies
100g butter, softened,
    or sour cream
bunch of fresh
    coriander, chopped

LEMON AND ROSEMARY CHICKEN

FOR THIS DISH YOU NEED TO FIND A SOURCE OF FRESH ROSEMARY – UNLESS, OF COURSE, YOU HAVE A BUSH IN YOUR OWN GARDEN.

Here's how...

Strip the rosemary sprigs bare, keeping the stalks. Chop half the leaves with the garlic and add the lemon zest. The remaining rosemary leaves can be used for another recipe or dropped on to the barbecue coals.

Skewer the diced chicken on the rosemary sticks and roll them in the chopped rosemary and garlic mix. Drizzle with olive oil plus a squeeze of lemon juice.

Grill on the barbecue for 10–12 minutes until firm. Serve in a pocket of grilled pitta bread stuffed with salad and sour cream. Season with salt and pepper.

Ingredients

Serves four

8 large rosemary
    sprigs
4 garlic cloves
zest and juice of
    2 lemons
4 free range chicken
    breasts, skinned
    and diced
olive oil
4 pitta breads
2 handfuls mixed
    salad
4 tbsp sour cream
salt and freshly
    ground black
    pepper

VEGETARIAN PAELLA

VEGETARIANS TEND TO FIGHT SHY OF BARBECUES,
SO HERE'S ANOTHER DISH JUST FOR THEM.

Here's how...

Heat the olive oil on the barbecue
in a paella dish or heavy-based
saucepan. Add the garlic, onion and
green and red peppers and fry until
they soften.

Add the thyme, chilli flakes and
paella rice, stirring until all the
grains of rice are nicely coated
and glossy.

Add the paprika, turmeric and dry
white wine. When it is bubbling, add
the vegetable stock little by little,
stirring continuously, and cook for
15–20 minutes until the rice is al
dente and the liquid is absorbed.

Sprinkle in the peas and chopped
tomatoes and continue to cook
gently for another 10 minutes.

Scatter the chopped parsley over
the paella, season and serve
immediately with wedges of lime.

Ingredients

Serves four

75ml good olive oil
2 garlic cloves, finely chopped
1 large Spanish onion, finely diced
2 green peppers, diced
2 red peppers, diced
1 tsp soft thyme leaves
1 tsp dried red chilli flakes
250g paella rice
2 tsp smoked paprika
1 tsp turmeric
125ml dry white wine
1.2 litres vegetable stock, heated
    with ½ tsp saffron strands
110g fresh or frozen peas
4 large tomatoes, de-seeded
    and chopped
5 tbsp chopped flat leaf parsley
salt and freshly ground
    black pepper
2 limes

SOMETHING SPECIAL

SATURDAY NIGHT. PARTY GEAR ON.
TIME TO SHOW YOUR BEST SIDE!

137

The best part of a dinner party for me is doing the cooking and (hopefully) wowing my guests with something new and exciting. But nobody wants to be stuck in the kitchen for hours before the guests arrive - so these recipes are designed to do the trick without too much fuss and bother.

CANAPÉS
WHY NOT START THE EVENING WITH A SELECTION
OF SURPRISING CANAPÉS? THESE SHOULD
GET THE CONVERSATION GOING...

PARMA HAM AND ROASTED ASPARAGUS

Ingredients

12 young asparagus
    spears
6 slices Parma ham
2 tbsp olive oil
freshly ground black
    pepper

Here's how...

Snap off the tender upper part of each asparagus and place in salted boiling water for 3 minutes. Then plunge the spears into icy cold water to stop the cooking process. When they are cool, leave to drain on kitchen paper.

Wrap half a slice of Parma ham around each asparagus spear, place on a baking tray and drizzle with olive oil. Season with pepper. Roast at 180°C for 10 minutes or so until the ham is crisp.

CHILLI VODKA CHERRY TOMATOES

Ingredients

3 red chillies
500ml vodka
12 cherry tomatoes

Here's how...

This recipe is incredibly simple but you do have to make the chilli vodka well in advance. Simply split two chillies down the middle and pop them into a bottle with the vodka. It'll take a day or two for the flavour to be absorbed. You won't need all the vodka but it will keep until next time or use it for Bloody Mary cocktails.

The day before your party, prick each of the tomatoes five or six times with a pin, split another chilli as before and place it with the tomatoes in a bowl. Add 150ml of the vodka to cover and leave overnight. Serve on cocktail sticks or in teaspoons.

HAGGIS AND WHISKY EN CROÛTE

Ingredients

100g puff pastry
250g haggis
2 egg yolks
4 tbsp whisky
sea salt

Here's how...

Start by rolling out a strip of puff pastry, 10 x 30cm. Break up the haggis and shape it into 12 small flat burger shapes. Line them up on half the pastry, about 2cm from the edge nearest you, leaving a 2–3cm gap between each one. Brush the pastry with egg yolk around the haggis.

Using a teaspoon, add a wee nip of whisky to each portion of haggis. Fold the puff pastry from the far edge towards you and seal up the haggis, using your finger to push out all the air. With a knife – or pasta wheel – cut round each haggis to make small squares. Finally brush with egg yolk and sprinkle a little sea salt on the top of each parcel.

Bake for 10 minutes at 200°C until golden brown.

KING SCALLOPS WITH SWEET POTATO PURÉE

THE KEY TO THIS RECIPE IS SOURCING SCALLOPS THAT ARE FIRM, PURE WHITE AND FRESH. I'M LUCKY TO HAVE A FISHMONGER WHO SUPPLIES SCALLOPS FROM JUST NORTH OF THE BORDER IN SCOTLAND.

Here's how...

Add the curry powder to the vegetable or groundnut oil and leave for a couple of minutes to let the spices infuse. This makes the curry oil used to cook and dress the scallops.

Preheat the oven to 200°C and bake the sweet potatoes for 30 minutes to 1 hour depending on size. While the potatoes are cooking, prepare the scallops by trimming off the orange roe. It's okay to eat the roes, but I like to dry them out in the oven and grind them down to powder to use as a natural pepper for seasoning fish dishes. Place the trimmed scallops on a tray lined with kitchen paper to absorb any water they might have soaked up during storage. Set aside.

Halve the cooked potatoes and allow to cool slightly. Scoop out the flesh and place in a saucepan. Add a teaspoon of ground cumin and a splash of cream. Mash, stir well, set aside and keep warm.

Pick the coriander leaves and chop the spring onions finely, placing them in a small bowl. Add some curry oil and stir so that all the leaves are dressed as you would a salad.

To cook the scallops, place a frying pan on the heat and leave to get really hot. Season the scallops with salt and pepper. Drizzle a few drops of curry oil onto each scallop and then place them into the hot frying pan. After about 30 seconds add the butter. Turn the scallops over and turn off the heat.

While you dress the plates, the scallops will continue to cook. Spoon out the sweet potato into three small quenelles (spoon-shaped servings), top each with a scallop and some dressed salad. Finish with more of the curry oil and serve.

Ingredients

Serves four

1 tbsp curry powder
100ml vegetable or groundnut oil
2 large sweet potatoes
12 diver-caught king scallops
1 tsp cumin
50ml double cream
handful of fresh coriander leaves
2 spring onions
salt and freshly ground black pepper
50g butter

PORCINI AND ROAST GARLIC SOUP

FOR THIS RECIPE I'VE COMBINED LOCALLY SOURCED WILD MUSHROOMS WITH A DASH OF ITALIAN FLAIR.

Here's how...

Place the garlic bulb in an ovenproof dish and drizzle with olive oil. Cook the garlic in the oven for 30 minutes at 170°C to soften and roast. You can do more than one of these bulbs at a time and preserve them in a jar topped up with olive oil.

Slice the shallots or onions and two garlic cloves. In a saucepan, cook the shallots, garlic, thyme, rosemary and potato in oil for 3–4 minutes until the shallots start to soften. Add the diced mushrooms and cook for a further 2 minutes.

Pour in the wine and reduce by half. Add the stock and cream and allow to simmer for 10–15 minutes until the potato is cooked. Season with salt and pepper.

Blend in a food processor. Pour into a bowl and serve with three or four of the roasted garlic cloves plus a little of the oil in which they were cooked.

Ingredients

Serves four

1 bulb garlic, plus
   2 extra cloves
20ml olive oil, plus
   extra for drizzling
4 banana shallots or
   2 small white onions
1 large sprig thyme
1 large sprig rosemary
½ potato
200g porcini
   mushrooms or ceps
1 large glass dry
   white wine
600ml vegetable stock
150ml double cream
salt and freshly ground
   black pepper

COCKTAIL SORBETS

THESE SORBETS ARE DESIGNED TO
CLEANSE THE PALATE AND GIVE
EVERYONE A BREAK FOR CONVERSATION
BEFORE THE MAIN COURSE.
ALL THE RECIPES SERVE EIGHT.

GIN AND TONIC SORBET

Ingredients

250g sugar
450ml water
250ml strong
    gin and tonic
zest and juice of
    3 limes

Here's how...

Dissolve the sugar in the water in a saucepan over low heat. Pour this syrup into a bowl and allow to cool.

Add the gin and tonic as well as the lime zest and juice to the syrup and pour into a suitable tray for the freezer. Freeze, stirring every 30 minutes until solid.

If you are using an ice cream machine churn the mixture for 20 minutes and then place it in the freezer.

PIMMS SORBET

Ingredients

250g sugar
450g water
zest and juice of 1 orange
zest and juice of 2 lemons
8 large mint leaves
250ml Pimms
½ cucumber peeled,
    deseeded and diced

Here's how...

Dissolve the sugar in the water in a saucepan over low heat. Pour this syrup into a bowl and add the orange and lemon zest and juice and the chopped mint leaves. Allow to cool. Add the Pimms and pour through a sieve into an ice cream machine or a suitable tray for the freezer. Freeze, stirring every 30 minutes until solid.

Once the sorbet has frozen, place the cucumber in the bottom of a cocktail glass and top with a spoonful of the sorbet.

KIR ROYAL SORBET

Ingredients

250g sugar
450ml water
450ml sparkling
    white wine or
    champagne
3 tbsp lemon juice
70ml crème de
    cassis

Here's how...

The procedure is the same as for the gin and tonic sorbet, except that you add champagne, lemon juice and crème de cassis to the syrup.

MOJITO SORBET

Ingredients

250g sugar
450ml water
zest and juice of
    1 lemon
zest and juice of
    1 lime
15 mint leaves
150ml white rum

Here's how...

The procedure is the same as for the gin and tonic sorbet, except that you add lemon and lime zest and juice, chopped mint and white rum to the syrup.

Serve this sorbet in cocktail glasses topped with fresh mint.

LOCAL VENISON WITH POTATO FONDANT AND PORT AND JUNIPER SAUCE

FORTUNATELY MORE AND MORE COUNTRY BUTCHERS NOW SELL VENISON. IT'S LEAN, TASTY AND VERY EASY TO COOK.

Here's how...

Start by chopping the rosemary and crushing the juniper berries with the base of a pan. Scatter over the venison, add a drizzle of olive oil and the honey and rub the marinade in. Leave for an hour or so.

Sauce For the sauce, place the chopped shallots, rosemary, juniper berries and butter in a large pan. Cook for a few minutes until the shallots have softened and you start to smell the aroma of the rosemary.

Add the port, red wine and sugar and reduce by half (in other words, boil until half the liquid has evaporated) . Add the beef stock and reduce again by half. Leave to one side until needed.

Potato fondant For the fondant, cut off the top and bottom of the potatoes so that they stand upright, then use a pastry cutter to cut out a central round portion from each.

Rub a little olive oil on to the tops of the potatoes and place them oil side down in a hot frying pan. Cook for about 5 minutes until golden brown, turn and transfer to an ovenproof dish. Pour the white wine and stock into the dish, then add the thyme and butter. Season with salt and pepper and cook in the oven for 45 minutes at 180°C.

Remove the venison from the marinade and season. Heat a heavy bottomed frying pan, add a splash of olive oil and brown the venison on all sides. Remove from the heat and place in the oven for 8 to 10 minutes. When it is cooked leave to rest under some foil.

Finally, warm the sauce and serve with the venison and potatoes.

Ingredients
Serves four

1 large sprig rosemary
10 juniper berries
800g tender loin venison
1 tbsp oilve oil
3 tbsp honey
salt and freshly ground
    black pepper

Sauce

2 shallots
sprig of rosemary
4 juniper berries
30g butter
100ml port
200ml red wine
1 tsp sugar or honey
200ml beef stock

Potato fondant

4 large potatoes
50ml olive oil
1 glass white wine
300ml vegetable stock
sprig of thyme
50g butter
salt and freshly ground
    black pepper

FILLET OF SALMON WITH ROASTED LEMON AND SAMPHIRE

A PERFECT LIGHT COMBINATION FOR A SUMMER DINNER PARTY.

Here's how...

Place a pan of salted water on the heat to boil. Season the salmon with salt, pepper and fennel seeds on both sides and drizzle with a little olive oil. Place the salmon skin-side down on a preheated grill pan and cook for 5 minutes

Slice the lemons in half and place cut-side down on the grill pan with the salmon. Turn the salmon over and cook for a further 3–4 minutes. The lemons caramelise and sweeten while the salmon cooks.

When the salmon and lemons are cooked, remove from the heat and leave to rest.

Place the samphire into the boiling water and cook for no more than 2 minutes. Check if the samphire is cooked by tasting a piece – it should be tender and taste a little of the sea.

Drain the samphire and add a knob of butter. Finally, squeeze the roasted lemon over the salmon and samphire. Serve with boiled or sautéed new potatoes.

Chef's Tip Samphire is one of Mother Nature's gifts but it is only available in early summer, so when it's in season and available, don't miss it. It tastes fantastic!

Ingredients
Serves four

4 x 250g salmon
   fillets
salt and freshly
   ground black
   pepper
½ tsp fennel
   seeds
4 tbsp olive oil
2 lemons
400g samphire
   (or asparagus if
   samphire is not
   in season)
knob of butter

OPEN LASAGNE WITH WILD MUSHROOMS

THIS DISH USES A SINGLE SHEET OF LASAGNE AS A WRAP ROUND THE ROASTED MUSHROOM. IT'S A TECHNIQUE THAT MAKES THE MOST OF THE MUSHROOM FLAVOUR.

Here's how...

Brush the mushrooms to ensure there is no soil left on them. Cut one clove of garlic into little spikes and push them into the caps of the mushrooms. Do the same with a few of the rosemary leaves and drizzle a little olive oil over the mushrooms. Place the mushrooms into the oven for 15 minutes to cook.

Boil a large pan of salted water and pour in the olive oil. This helps to prevent the lasagne from sticking. Add the lasagne sheets. Fresh lasagne will take only 2–3 minutes to cook, dried about 9–10 minutes.

While the pasta and mushrooms are cooking sauté the shallots and remaining garlic and rosemary in a little olive oil until softened. Add the brandy and cream and reduce (boil down) by half. Season to taste, set aside and keep warm.

When the lasagne is cooked, remove from the water and place in a bowl with a little olive oil to prevent it from sticking.

Lay a sheet of lasagne on each plate, sit a mushroom on it and fold it over. Place another mushroom on top of that and fold over again. Spoon the sauce over the pasta and serve.

Ingredients

Serves four

8 Portobello or large
   field mushrooms
2 cloves garlic
2 large sprigs
   rosemary
20 ml olive oil, plus
   extra for drizzling
   and cooking
4 sheets fresh
   lasagne
2 shallots
50ml brandy
100ml double cream
salt and freshly
   ground black
   pepper

CARAMELISED SHALLOT AND GOAT'S CHEESE TATIN

AN UPSIDE-DOWN TART THAT BLENDS THE RICHNESS OF GOAT'S CHEESE WITH THE SWEETNESS OF CARAMELISED SHALLOTS.

Here's how...

Peel the shallots and sauté in an ovenproof frying pan with the butter and thyme. When they have softened and gained some colour add the balsamic vinegar and sugar. Reduce the heat and allow to cook for 20 minutes or so on a low heat. Season and leave to cool.

Roll out the puff pastry into a circular shape to fit the same frying pan. If you want to make the tarte tatin in smaller, individual pans, adapt the size of the pastry shapes accordingly.

When the shallots have cooled, lay the pastry over the pan and tuck in the edges to make sure the shallots are all covered. Brush the pastry with a little egg yolk and bake for 15 minutes at 185°C .

When the pastry is golden brown, remove from the oven and leave to cool. Run a knife round the edge of the pan and flip the tart over. It should just drop out, but if a few of the shallots have stuck don't worry – just peel them off and put them back where they should be.

Cut four slices of goat's cheese and place on top of the tart. Return the tart to a hot oven for 5 minutes or so until the cheese is golden.

Serve with rocket leaves dressed with aged balsamic vinegar (preferably a 12-year-old vinegar if you can get one).

Ingredients

Serves four

8 large or banana
    shallots
50g butter
sprig of thyme
100ml balsamic
    vinegar
4 tbsp sugar
salt and freshly ground
    black pepper
400g puff pastry
2 egg yolks
4 slices (300g) soft
    rind goat's cheese
    log
2 handfuls rocket
    leaves
aged balsamic vinegar,
    to serve

COFFEE BEFORE DESSERT
DON'T BE FOOLED BY THE PICTURE, THIS IS A
SOPHISTICATED SIGNATURE DISH, NOT A CAPPUCCINO.

Here's how...

Custard Start by making a custard. Separate the
eggs and place the yolks and sugar in a bowl,
then whisk them together until light and fluffy.

Run a knife down the half vanilla pod and split it
open. Place the cream and milk in a saucepan
with the vanilla pod and bring to the boil.
Gradually add to the whisked egg yolks, pour
the mixture back into the saucepan and leave to
one side.

Melt the chocolate in a bowl in the microwave in
20 second bursts. When it has melted, add the
butter, espresso and cream and mix together.

Pour the mixture into four coffee cups and place
in the fridge to set. When you are ready to serve,
simply warm up the custard, froth with a hand
blender and spoon on to the top of each cup.

Ingredients
Serves four

100g dark
    chocolate
50g butter
4 x 35ml shots of
    espresso coffee
300ml double
    cream

Custard
2 egg yolks
30g caster sugar
½ vanilla pod
150ml double
    cream
150ml milk

CHOCOLATE AND ORANGE FONDANT WITH CINNAMON ICE CREAM

NO DINNER PARTY MENU WOULD BE COMPLETE WITHOUT A CHOCOLATE CREATION, SO HERE'S ONE OF MY FAVOURITES.

Here's how...

Rub a little butter round the inside of four ramekin moulds, then dust the inside with a coating of cocoa powder. The easy way is to pour cocoa powder from one dish to the next until they are all coated.

Melt the chocolate in a large bowl over a saucepan of simmering water, add the butter and orange zest. When the chocolate is melted, whisk the eggs, yolks and sugar together until pale and light then add to the chocolate and mix well.

Next, sieve the flour into the mix and fold it in. Spoon the mixture into each of the moulds and tap them on your worktop once or twice just to settle the contents.

Place in the oven for 12 minutes at 160°C. When they are cooked run a knife round the edge and remove from the dishes.

For the ice cream, save time by using a tub of your favourite vanilla. Allow to soften, stir in the cinnamon and return to the freezer until needed.

Chef's Tip Make an extra portion to use for testing – just in case.

Ingredients

Serves four

100g butter, plus extra for greasing
4 tbsps cocoa powder
100g dark chocolate (70% cocoa)
zest of 1 orange
2 eggs plus 2 extra yolks
120g sugar
100g plain flour
500ml vanilla ice cream
½ tsp cinnamon

APPLE CRUMBLE PARFAIT WITH CARAMELISED APPLES

THIS RECIPE TRANSFORMS A POPULAR ENGLISH
CLASSIC INTO A SOPHISTICATED FROZEN DESSERT.

Here's how...

Place the flour and butter in a bowl and rub together with your fingertips to create a crumble. Add the golden sugar and cinnamon, mix together and place on a baking tray. Bake for 20 minutes at 170°C until golden and crisp

Peel, core and chop four of the apples and blend in a food processor with the lemon juice. If you don't have a food processor simply grate the apples into a bowl.

Pour the blended apples into a sieve to drain through into a bowl. Separate the eggs into a bowl of whites and a bowl of yolks. Heat 250ml of the cream in a saucepan on a low heat and, in a separate bowl, whisk the egg yolks and 100g caster sugar together until light and fluffy.

When the cream just starts to simmer pour it into the whisked egg yolks and mix together. Leave aside to cool.

To make the meringue, whisk the egg whites with a pinch of salt, gradually adding the remaining caster sugar a little at a time until the egg whites are quite stiff and form soft peaks.

Lastly, whisk the remaining double cream so that it just starts to thicken. You now have each part of the dish ready to mix.

Ingredients

Serves four

200g flour
125g butter
60g golden or
    demerara sugar
1 tsp cinnamon
6 Granny Smith apples
juice of 1 lemon
6 eggs
500ml double cream
200g caster sugar,
    plus extra to taste
pinch of salt
1 cinnamon stick
4 tbsp apple brandy

Continues over page

Start by adding the drained apple juice to the egg yolk mix and stirring together. Add the whipped double cream and mix well. Finally fold in the meringue.

Line a loaf tin with cling film, spoon in half of the crumble and spread it evenly across the base. Pour in the apple mix, leaving space at the top for the remaining crumble.

When the tin is full just give it a tap to remove any air pockets and freeze overnight.

Peel the remaining two apples and cut into eight. Heat a frying pan and add the apples and cinnamon stick. Add sugar to taste if required and cook on a medium heat until the apples start to take on a caramel colour. Add the apple brandy and remove from the heat.

To serve, remove the parfait from the freezer about 10 minutes before it is needed and run a long knife under a hot tap so that it is easier to cut into nice clean portions.

Arrange on a plate with the warm caramelised apples and decorate with a piece of cinnamon stick. You'll find the two contrasting temperatures work really well together.

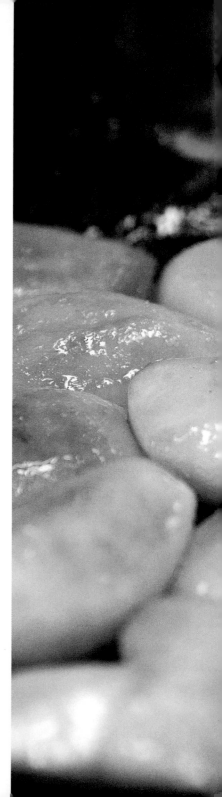

BLUE CHEESE MARINATED WITH PORT AND WALNUTS

I CAME UP WITH THIS IDEA WHILE TALKING TO ONE OF MY CHEFS ABOUT FLAVOURING STILTON CHEESE WITH PORT AT CHRISTMAS TIME. IT STARTED ME THINKING ABOUT DIFFERENT WAYS OF DOING IT…

Here's how...

You will need to make sure your local cheesemonger or butcher has a vacuum packing machine and they would not mind sealing a bag for you.

Roast the walnuts in the oven on a baking tray for 10 minutes at 180°C so that they are really crunchy. Allow to cool and then push the roasted walnuts into the cheese.

Place the cheese in a vacuum bag and pour over a glass of vintage port. Take the bag of cheese down to your cheese shop or butcher and ask them to seal the bag for you.

Leave the bag in the fridge for a few days and… hey presto! Port marinated Stilton. Serve with digestive biscuits or oatcakes.

Ingredients

Serves four

75g walnuts
300g Stilton or
    local blue cheese
150ml port

WHITE CHOCOLATE ICE CREAM WITH GRASMERE GINGERBREAD

HERE'S A QUICK FIX IF YOU WANT AN ALTERNATIVE TO TRUFFLES OR MINTS AS A FINALE FOR YOUR DINNER PARTY.

Here's how...

Soften the ice cream and grate in the white chocolate. Stir and refreeze.

Place a scoop of ice cream on each of four dessertspoons and arrange on a serving plate. Top with gingerbread crumbs (I prefer our local Grasmere gingerbread) and orange zest.

Just for good measure, I've left enough to spare in the ingredients for second helpings!

Ingredients

Serves four

500ml vanilla ice
    cream
100g white chocolate
2 large gingerbread
    biscuits, crumbled
zest of 1 orange

Conversions

Oven Temperatures

°C	°F	Gas Mark	Oven
140	275	1	Cool
150	300	2	
170	325	3	Moderate
180	350	4	
190	375	5	Moderately Hot
200	400	6	
220	425	7	Hot
230	450	8	
240	475	9	Very Hot

Liquid Measurements

5ml	1 teaspoon (tsp)
10ml	1 dessertspoon (dsp)
15ml	1 tablespoon (tbsp) or ½ fl oz
30ml	1 fl oz
60ml	2 fl oz
75ml	2½ fl oz
100ml	3½ fl oz
150ml	5 fl oz (¼ pt)
300ml	½ pt
450ml	¾ pt
600ml	1 pt (20 fl oz)
1 litre	1¾ pt

Weights

15g	½ oz
25g	1 oz
50g	2 oz
75g	3 oz
110g	4 oz (¼ lb)
150g	5 oz
175g	6 oz
200g	7 oz
225g	8 oz (½ lb)
250g	9 oz
275g	10 oz
300g	11 oz
350g	12 oz (¾ lb)
375g	13 oz
400g	14 oz
425g	15 oz
450g	16 oz (1 lb)
500g	1 lb 2 oz
675g	22 oz (1½ lb)
1kg	2¼ lb

All conversions
are approximate

Acknowledgements

For their help and support with writing this book I would like to thank my wife Emma, daughter Poppy and all my family – Mum, Dad, Andrew, Harriet Rose, Annabelle May, Brenda and Richard.

Thanks go to my food stylist and café manager, Kylie Overton, to my chefs Dan Grimshaw, Danny Hartley and Becca Newton and to all the staff of *Good Taste* for looking after the café while I was working on the book.

A special 'thank you' goes to James, Fiona and Jack Breedon for their encouragement and to all my loyal customers and friends at *Good Taste*. Without them there would be no book.

My thanks go to John Walker and Deborah Cowin at *The Necessary Angel* for convincing me to write a cookery book, Stuart Holmes for contributing the Lake District landscape photography, and *The Keswick Area Partnership* for their backing.

I am also grateful to John Kinsella, Duncan, Trish and Matt Overton, Diane and John Shaw, Penny Turnbull, Linda and Tosh Martin, Tina Smith, Fiona and Douglas, *Thomasons Butchers* and *The FondEwe Cheese Shop*, Keswick.

Peter Sidwell

Images of The Lakes

Stuart Holmes

The Lakeland images in this book are the work of acclaimed local photographer Stuart Holmes, who was brought up in Keswick and returned to live there after working in Europe, Africa and the Middle East as an exploration geologist.

'For me it's the perfect adventure playground; I can run, bike, climb, fly and swim within this stunning landscape, all within a stone's throw of my front door,' he says.

As a photojournalist specialising in adventure sports and travel, Stuart has contributed to numerous magazines including Cumbria and Lake District Magazine, The Countryman, HIGH, Cycling Today, Global Adventure, Amateur Photographer, Men's Health and even Mayfair (a photo essay on ice climbing).

After business and pleasure forays to Turkmenistan, Nepal, Patagonia and South Georgia he joined a group of friends on a low budget private expedition to Tibet and reached the summit of Mount Everest at 6 a.m. on 30th May, 2005.

Stuart's images can be found on pages 7, 11 and 13.

Stuart Holmes
www.sharpedgeimages.co.uk